T0209189

IMPRESSIONS
in the
WATER

NORMAN CARTER

BALBOA.
PRESS

A DIVISION OF HAY HOUSE

Balboa Press books may be ordered through booksellers or by contacting:

Balboa Press
A Division of Hay House
1663 Liberty Drive
Bloomington, IN 47403
www.balboapress.com
1 (877) 407-4847

Print information available on the last page.

ISBN: 978-1-9822-1290-2 (sc)
ISBN: 978-1-9822-1291-9 (e)

Balboa Press rev. date: 02/27/2019

Contents

Acknowledgments

First and foremost, thank you Lord for using me as the vessel to allow your anointing to flow through and bless your people. For that, I am eternally grateful. Thank you for your spiritual inspiration and revelation.

Special thanks to Adilia Martinez for her professionalism in editing.

Impressions In The Water

As He gazed upon the waters still
He saw mountains, and valleys, and rolling hills
In the gardens He so majestically aligned
There were flowers on stems, and shrubs, and vines
Reds, and pinks, and violets, and blue
Gardenias, tulips, and daffodils too
He saw fruit trees filled with earthly delights
That would flood one's mouth with every bite
Suspended in time and struck with awe
He was amazed as He gazed at the things He saw
But when He looked into His silhouette
There He saw no reflection, yet!
He saw winds kissing the trees, as they brushed against the sky
With shallow breath and a tear in His eye
I asked, "what's wrong my Lord, what could it be
Are You not pleased with the things You see"?
He said, oh no my soul, heavens no
I see Myself in the clouds, some as white as snow
There's stratus, and altocumulus, and cirrostratus, and more
There are cumulus funnels that would reach heavens floor
And return with lightening, and a thunderous' roar
With turbulent storms that would shake the earth's very core
Rushing waves with their chest stuck high
Crashing the shores just to say, I, I

Over, and over, and over again
Adorned in white caps, and bowing in the sand
O yes, the sand, amassed in numbers, who can count?
What could I've been thinking about?
On one shore it's fine, and fluffy, and white like snow
And on another, its course, and yellow, and all aglow
And yet another, it's gritty, and sharp, and black as jet
And that's just the beginning, I'm not finished yet
That's just the beginning, who knew
Earth! Open your belly, open wide
Show forth the treasures that I hide
There's jasper, onyx, and sapphire too
Carbuncles, rubies, and diamonds true
Tremulously gleaming in whites, yellows, and blue
Oh no My soul, displeased, couldn't be
Such brilliance and grandeur created by Me
Even the soft green grasses spring up to meet Me as I kneel
With outstretched arms, waters, be still
Majestic creatures, thyself reveal
There are dolphins, and porpoises, and huge blow whales
Starfish and seahorses, and tuna assail
I see the eel, and the stingray, and all the fishes of the sea
While the fouls of the air assemble around Me
Consider the splendor of the butterfly, beauty untold
Born a worm, then unfold
The entire spectrum, thy colors divine
I in him and he is mine
Or black and yellow, the bumble bee
How they fly, defying gravity
Displeased, I don't dare
My magnificence, to what may I compare

How about weightless insects that ride on the air?
Or birds gliding through the sky without a care
And the eagle, able to fly straightway into the sun
Or the speed of a cheetah, on a flat-out run
Oh, I see Myself in My animals, and how they abound
The giraffe reaching skyward
Or the mole tunneling under ground
The trumpet of the elephant
And the pitch of his sound
The stealthiness of the leopard
As he pounces on his pray
Or, the grace of the gazelle, as he springs away
Of all that I've created, I'm very pleased
Yet, still I on bended knees
Something is missing
What could it be?
After all, I Am Elohim
The Creator of all things
I spoke to darkness, and created light
Called one day, and the other night
I separated on earth, the waters from on high
The divider I used, I called the sky
And every living thing I've created, reproduces from inside
In the form of seeds, where life I hide
I created the sun and the moon out of light
One to rule over the day, and the other to rule over the night
From the gleam in my eyes, came the stars
There's Saturn, Jupiter, Pluto, and Mars
Orion, the Dippers, and the Milky Way
They lead by night, and hide by day

Slowly rising, with His legs standing wide, and
a grin on His face, bursting with pride
Peering upward, with His arms crossing His chest
He said "this is good, I think I'll rest."

Who Is Man?

Lord, who is man, that You created with such care
You gave him the earth, and placed him there
You created everything, without a single touch
You spoke to the universe, and it obeyed as much
Harkening to Your voice, bringing before Your face
Molecules and atoms, through time, and space
Aligning themselves perfectly in place
After six days you decided to rest
For Your next creation would be your very best
Architect of the universe
Grand master of the day
Ground for Your canvas, with palette' of clay
Your next creation
Even the universe couldn't produce
So, no other words You spoke
For there was no use
From the dust of the ground, with Your bare hands
Gathering, and shaping, You molded a man
Twisting and sculpting, tenacious and hue
Created in the image and likeness of You
O my Myself, is this really Me
Erect and muscular, handsome as could be
So moved with emotions, and misty with glee
He said, for the very first time, My face I see

All that I'd commanded of time and space
Were mere expressions of Me, but not My face
The Lord stood looking, eye to eye
With a love so deep, He began to cry
Then, gathering Himself, with gentle inhale
He breathed into Man's nostrils, His spirit expelled
In that very moment, man became a living being
Walking, and talking, and thinking, and seeing
Placed in the Garden, there to reside
Knowing that from The Lord, he'd never have to hide
Son, the Lord said, in a peremptory voice
This garden I give you, and even a choice
All that you see, with love, I freely give
Now in lasting peace, I bid you, live.

The Garden

Now, living in the garden, what a thrill
Adam, enjoying life, of his own free will
All he'd ever need was an arm's length away
living in bliss, every day
An ambrosial fragrance the garden did yield
With rose petal carpet, under his heels
There were plants and trees of every kind
Water for drinking, and grapes for wine
Occasionally the Lord came to visit his man
To give him instructions, and share his plan
Everything in the garden, eat as much
But in the mist, there's a tree, you must not touch
Adam walked through his habitat, peaceful and serene
With nothing to do, not even a song to sing
Looking from a distance the Lord could see
That His greatest creation was lonely as could be
So, He herded the animals one by one
And told him to name them, just for fun
Adam christened the rabbits, and the squirrels, and the foxes, and the bears
The hyenas, the pachyderms, and the birds in the air
Then came the lizards, and the frogs, and the beavers, and the hogs
The cattle and the chipmunks, and the cats, and the dogs
The designation he gave them, were after their kind
And that appellation would last until the end of time

When he had finished naming them all
Again, his demeanor began to fall
For out of all the animals there was no help meet
So, the Lord decided to put him to sleep
He needs someone special, the Lord would say
Someone to be with him night and day
Someone to show him, himself inside
And expose those emotions that he'll try to hide
Someone that he could love, as deeply as I love him
That he'd nurture, and provide for, and even die, in a whim
Someone soft, and gentle, and under control
Who'd delight his eyes with beauty untold
Rounded with curves, and crowned with hair
To please his palate, and demand his stare
Unlike Man, from the dust of the ground, this jewel couldn't hide
So, the Lord wounded the man and took her from his inside
Being quite pleased with what He had done,
He awakened Adam from his sleep
Stretching and yawning, he took a peep
Standing over him in quintessence
He gazed upon her beauty in its true essence
Immediately his eyes opened wide, and he leaped to his feet
Around in a circle for a panoramic view, pacing
to and fro not knowing what to do
His heart was pounding heavily, and his blood beginning to rush
Barely able to breathe and filling kind of blushed
So engrossed with emotions that were all too new
He summoned the Lord, because he didn't know what to do
Oh my Lord, could this be
You've created this amazing creature for me
Adam, this is Eve

I created her to be your help meet
And for all times to come, to you she'll cleave
The wound in your side, I took her from there
To be protected under your arms, and in your council, and care
And when life's challenges weigh you down
She'll offer her breast, where comfort is found
And if ever in life you should come up slack
Not to worry, she'll have your back
She'll bear your children, raise them up
And make you very proud
She'll honor your name in the market place
Even before the crowds
Forsaking all, love her, provide for her, protect
her, and of yourself, freely give
And you, twine, in harmony shall live.

P.S. Debra, I dedicate this poem to you on Valentine's Day. God entrusted you to me, to Love, and provide for, and protect, and even to die for if need be. To this I say thank you Lord, I accept my responsibility.

I love you

Norman

The Great Fall

Now in the garden, Adam and Eve
Living their lives as free as a breeze
Spending their days in harmony
Lavishly living without frugality
Adams behavior was becoming reason for concern
He was losing his focus, and ability to discern
Bone of my bone, flesh of my flesh
He was so enamored by her beauty, he was becoming a mess
The way he followed her around, like bees after honey
Even the Lord must have thought it funny
From the balcony of heaven, the Father said
He's losing his focus, he's being led
Her amore and symmetry has gotten him in a pickle
The way he follows her around, acting kind of fickled
Walking in the garden naked, and unashamed
Is causing him to slip
And lose his reign
I created him to be the head, and to lead the way
But he's losing ground, every day
There must be an intervention, if my plan is to resume
The way he's going, he's headed for doom
Among all that He'd created, looking back
Seeking a way to get Adam on track
The Lord saw the serpent, the most cunning of all his creatures

Slow walking, smooth talking, and possessing all the right features
You'll do, was the Lords recant
The price will be steep, but the woman you must enchant
One particular day, Eve was walking through the garden
Picking choice fruits for their afternoon meal
Adam was there with her, right on her heels
Out in the distance something caught her stare
Undulating towards her, looking debonair
Walking on all fours until he'd gotten rather close
It was that captivating serpent that had her engrossed
Reaching for the tree he began his ascent
When at a comfortable height, his case he'd present
Out on a limb he did slither, extending his torso with acrobat
Then lending himself to Eve, as close as he could get
With calculation, and tongue a hiss
With his eyes piercing hers, he said: Eve, listen to this
Has God indeed said, from every tree, you may enjoy a treat?
She glanced back at Adam for solace to be heard
But he didn't open his mouth, didn't mutter a word
For a brief moment she recalled instructions given by her head
While in the entanglement of the serpent she said
Of every tree, we may eat as much
But this tree, we must not touch!
With one suave swipe, the serpent removed a piece of fruit from the tree
And brought it into view for Eve to see
"What do you suppoozze would happen", was hizzz reply
She said "if we eat from this tree we'll surely die"
Circling her face, looking upside down
Turning his smile into a frown
Rubbing the fruit as he regressed
Making it look it's very best

Recoiling to strike his final blow
"Surely you won't die if this fruit you bite
What will happen izzz, your eyes will be opened
And you'll know good from evil, and wrong from right"
In one fatal move the serpent sprang pass Eve to confront her man
Simultaneously offering her the fruit in his hand
Distracting Adam to give insight
Meanwhile the woman was taking a bite
"Adam, I've seen you, following her around, feeling all erotic
She's leading you by the nose, looking all exotic
Not to worry, that'll all change after you take a bite"
Handing him the fruit after eating her fill
He did accept it, of his own free will
"Go ahead Adam, take a bite
You'll be leading her erroneously before midnight"
Totally succumbed in utter defeat
In one climatic moment, he did eat
Immediately his eyes filled with tears, and his heart filled with shame
Knowing full well what he'd done, and where he'd place the blame
With empty feelings no longer able to look each other eye to eye
Their hearts still breaking, they both began to cry
Experiencing uncontrollable sadness and being filled with lament
Smelling the stench of sin, an ungodly scent
They mourned all day in total regret
Not having dealt with their nakedness yet
They took fig leaves and wrapped them around
Then hid behind the trees so they wouldn't be found.

Evicted

In the cool of the evening the Lord took a stroll
To restore order, that Adam might regain control
Considering to himself as He walked along
The events of the day and what had gone wrong
I put before him the tree of knowledge, and warned if he touched it
That he'd surely die
Yet, at the word of that serpent, he did eat, knowing full well it was a lie
The woman eating from the tree I understand
Her design was to be a help meet, and to submit only to her man
When she turned to him for his instructions to be heard
He didn't open his mouth, didn't say a word
Allowing that serpent to talk in his stead
Usurping his authority, taking his head
Was it because I'd supplied all his needs
And he had no experiences from which to glean?
If he had, from a distance, that snake he would have seen
For the first time so moved, yet my heart I must harden
I have no choice, but to evict them from the garden
For in the mist there remains the tree of life
If he partakes of it, he'll live forever in sin and strife
Summoning his strength after a long sigh
Girding his loins round about
With a chiding voice He began to shout
Adam, Adam, where are you

Slowly they emerged from behind the trees
With sadness preceding them
Knowing the Lord would not be pleased
We're here Lord, he said with a solemn voice
Behind the trees we hid our nakedness, we had no choice
Who told you, you were naked, surely not I?
You've eaten from the tree, now tell me, why?
To ashamed to accept responsibility, or take the blame
With a voice of low self-esteem his retort came
It was that woman you gave me
She handed me the fruit, and I did eat it
Yes, you did, and in your own domain you've been defeated
Woman, how could you do this thing?
It was the serpent by whom I was deceived
You were created to be a help meet, and to your husband only to cleave
Now the serpent stood leaning against the tree all the while
With his legs crossed, picking his nails, wearing a sanctimonious smile
To the serpent the Lord said; enjoy your smile while you can
For it's suddenly fleeting
From this day forward until the end of time
Dust you'll be eating
Until eternity has come and gone
On your belly you'll crawl
Beneath the feet of every beast you'll fall
Your eyes will be dimmed and your tongue I'll divide
Forever your mouth will taste of poison
Because out of it you've lied
Your lies have become the presage of man doing the same
But I'll send him the Holy Ghost, his tongue, He'll tame
Unto the woman He said, because of this thing you've done
Your pain and sorrows have just begun

In child bearing your pain will multiply
And many times, your heart will break
Because of a lie
Many of the lies you'll want to believe are true
For they'll come from your husband, who has rule over you
And to the man the Lord said
In spite of my instructions, you acknowledged the words your wife spoke
Because of what you've done, our covenant, you broke
From the fruits of this garden, you'll no longer partake
Cursed is this ground for your sake
By the sweat of your brow shall you toil
For thorns and thistles shall spring forth from the soil
You will eat from the herbs of the field
And the life that you're leaving will no longer be the same
Until you return to the dust, from whence you came.

Amen

Provisions After The Garden

Early in the morning the Lord stood
at the east end of the garden
Where Adam and Eve would soon be departing
Making decisions that only he could make
Banishing them from the garden for their own sakes
For in the mist there remains the tree of life
If they partook of it, they'd live forever, in sin and strife
Cursed is this ground, from which they feed
Cursed are the herbs, and cursed are their seeds
I've given them charge to replenish the earth
And have whatever they say
As they exit, I'll baptize them in water
And unto Me, they'll desire to pray
From out in the distance came the man and his wife
Sorrow covering them so thickly it could cut it with a knife
Just outside the garden entrance rain began to pour
This was an anomaly to the man
For he had never seen it before
One final step out of the garden and into the shower
He somehow knew from wince it came
And of its accompanying power
Looking back as he departed, he said
Even now Lord, after what I've done
You're showering me with love and hope, of things to come

Painfully that was all that he would muster to say
Then he turned and walked away
East of the Garden of Eden
God commanded cherubim to stand guard at the post
With flaming swords turning in every direction, warding off all host
A sniffle or so from the Lord, and the rain began to subside
God knowing forever more, from man, his face He must hide
He can never stand before me again
Because I have no part with sin
For now, life will take its course
But make no mistake about it, "I AM" the presiding voice
In its season I'll send a mediator, He'll be the Christ
Who will bring forth my word?
From the desert sands to the mountain tops
My voice will be heard
He'll come as a man, natural as can be
And take the sins of the world upon his shoulders
And hang them back on the tree
To the grave He'll carry them
And the number of days He'll terry will be three
When He rise, in His mouth will be the gospel
And in His hand will be the key
He'll raise up Apostles to lead the way
And Profits who'll proclaim what they've been given to say
Through the voice of the Evangelist
In the lands, over the highways, oceans and byways
My word will be heard
Knowledge, wisdom, and understanding will be shared by the teacher
Love, patients, and partition, will be ministered by the Preacher
Afterwards My Son, "The Christ" will return to Me
And He'll send you a comforter, you'll see

Inside of you He'll reside
He'll unction you, and prompt you, and tell you what to do
In this you'll know, my word is true.
Amen

Cain and Abel

Adam began to know his wife as quickly as he could
First, they bore a son named Cain, who wasn't very good
Cain was a farmer, a tiller of the ground
Next came Abel, a herdsman
He offered the Lord his very best
Cain kept the best of his harvest, and offered the Lord the rest
God respected Abel's offering
It was the fattest and the first
Because Cain only offered runts
Upon himself he brought a curse
When he saw that the Lord had accepted Abel's offering
It made him very mad
So, God came to him with council
Saying, Son it's not that bad
This is not the way to go, your attitude is poor
If you do well, you'll be accepted
If you don't, fear will be waiting at your door
Be willing to change, that's my will
If fear rules over you, it could cause you to kill
No sooner had the voice of the Lord departed
Cain lured his brother Abel into the field
There he rose up against him, and Abel's blood, he did spill
Soon the Lord approached him and asked, where is your brother Abel?
In a rude tone he replied, am I my brothers' keeper?

Maybe he's in the stable
The Lord grew angry because Cain had lied
I know what you've done
From the ground beneath the voice of your brothers' blood has cried
Because of what you've done, from the earth you are cursed
She'll no longer yield her bounty
When you hunger and when you thirst
You'll be a fugitive and a vagabond
And everywhere you go
You'll be mocked and scorned whenever your face you show
Cain now realizing his destiny and fate
Knowing that where ever he'd go, he'd be a victim of hate
Cain began to plead with the Lord
Lord, you've driven me from this ground
Now where ever my feet shall tread
For me, no peace will be found
Where ever I go no one will treat me fair
This burden that I've brought upon myself is more than I can bare
Even after what he'd done, the Lord heard his mercy cry
And out of his love for all mankind
He refused to let Cain die
Go your way son He said, I'll give you a mark to wear
And who ever attempts to take your life
Seven times your punishment, they'll bare
So, the Lord placed His mark on Cain
To keep his enemies away
Then Cain headed east of Eden
In the land of Nod is where he'd stay.

Cain On The Run

Cain took his sister with him, while on the run
In the land of Nod is where they settled
And there they had a son
They also built a city
Enoch was its name
He named it after his son, the beginning of the lineage of Cain
First, there was Enoch, he had a son name Irad
One of the many children he'd had
There was Mathujael, who fathered Mathusael
Then came Lamech, the first mentioned to take two wives
Adah and Zillah were their names
Adah bore Jabal, the maker of tents
Then she bore Jubal, the inventor of instruments
Zillah had a son, Tubal-Cain
He was a forge man, from which bronze instruments came
Meanwhile back at the ranch of Adam and Eve
Getting on with life, again she conceived
All to her dismay she began to pray
My God you've given me a son this day
I'll name him Seth, and he'll carry the soul of Abel
He'll call upon you, as his Lord and savior
Abel was the son whose blood was spilled
By the hands of his brother out in the field

As I live and breathe from this generation on
It'll be the name of the Lord that He'll call upon
Seth first son, Enos was his De plume
It was in his generation that worship was assumed.

The Generations From Adam To Noah

Seth was the third son of Adam, he carried his brother Abel's soul
It was in his lineage that worship began to unfold
This came about by the tithe given by Abel
Being acceptable to the Lord
He was granted favor
Seth it was that brought joy to the heart of Eve
At a ripe old age, she did conceive
And it filled her eyes with tears
At the age of one-hundred and thirty, Adam begat Seth
Then lived another eight hundred years
In the seventh generation was Enoch
It was he who never died
He worshiped in such a special way
The Lord took him up, to be by His side
Before the Lord took him away at the age of three hundred and sixty-five
He fathered Methuselah, who became the oldest man alive
Methuselah begat Lamech at the age of one hundred and eighty-seven
And he lived nine hundred and sixty-nine years, before he went to heaven
Lamech begat Noah, the tenth generation, at the age of eighty-two
Then lived another five hundred and ninety-five years
And the begats were finally through.

Noah and The Ark

Noah walked circumspect before the Lord
At a time when humanity was saturated with sin
And the lust of the flesh would assumingly win
Noah carried the intent of Adam
But with much more power
Adams redemption was assured
When he stepped out of the Garden
Into the shower
The beauty of women of that time
Must have been something to behold
It was in part the cause of Adams demise
And loss of control
Even during Noah's time
To what could their beauty compare
That would cause the Sons of God to look upon them
And regard them as fair
This and the wickedness of man grieved the Lord so
That his spirit would not tarry with man for long
Because of their ungodly ways, and continual wrong
Man had to go
So, the Lord decided to cause a rain and cleanse the face of the earth
Unharmonious behavior and continual wickedness
Had diminished man's worth
In this generation Noah walked with the Lord and found favor

It was his ancestors that worshipped the Lord
And claimed him as their savior
God instructed Noah to build an ark to specific specifications
It was to be done in the time allotted
Because He was going to destroy the nations
Noah took his sons, Shem, Ham, and Japheth, and told them what to do
And the Lord would gather the animals and bring them in two by two
It hadn't rained in the land for quite a while He said
But don't worry about what the people will say
They'll laugh and mock and scorn you, until the very last day
Let this be a lesson to you
It doesn't matter what people say
You continue to heed My voice and I will lead the way
No sooner had Noah finished building the Ark
Rain clouds began to roll in
And the skies began to grow very dark
Then the animal came marching in two by two
Just as the Lord promised He'd do
In came the elephants, the giraffes, the lions, and the bears
The pigs, the monkeys, and even the hares
Followed by dogs, the cats, the beavers, and the bats
The snakes, and the skunks, and the little chipmunks
After the Lord had harvested them all
Rain suddenly began to fall
Noah and his sons gathered to pray
They thanked the Lord for providing their way
Afterwards they went inside
Rain poured vehemently, and about the third day
Crowds of people were heading their way
Panic stricken and ready to believe
Without hope, and their hearts aggrieved
Noah closed the window, and walked away.

The Triumphant Entry

Jesus was fast approaching His final hour
Prayed up and filled up, from on high with power
As He neared the town of Bethany
The stage was set
and He was ready to go
The Lord allowed Him to make a grand entrance
And put on a show
Jesus sent two disciples into the village
For a colt to borrow
And told them to tell anyone who'd ask
That the Lord had need of it
And would return it tomorrow
Sure enough, as they entered the city
The first house they saw, there a colt was tied
One upon who's back, no man had ever taken a ride
They brought it back to Jesus per His request
A young virgin colt, the fattest and the best
Before Jesus sat upon it, to take His grand ride
They covered it with a garment
Then walked along its side
Out in the distance, they could see the gates of the city
And the gathering of the crowds
As they began to call upon the Lord
And Praise his name out loud

Hosanna, Hosanna, they began to sing

David is our Father, and Thou art his King

The choir ran out to meet Him carrying palm leaves

Overcome by His presence, some fell to their knees

Hosanna, Hosanna, was the praise for the hour

Jesus rode high, adorned in glory, and filled with power

They lay palm leaves before Him, and even

their coats as they gathered around

From the moment they met Him, until He reached the gates

His feet never touched the ground

Hosanna, Hosanna, rang like a battle cry

All Praises be to our Lord on high

Hosanna, Hosanna was the claim

Blessed be the Lord on high, from which our Savior came

They praised Him with all manner of prayer

Standing, bowing, dancing about

Some going before Him, others following, many breaking out into a shout

What a celebratory day, and a sight to behold

Jesus, entering the city of Jerusalem

On the back of a fold

Inside the city, after the celebration died down

Jesus headed to the Temple to take a look around

Realizing that the sun was fading, and they were losing daylight

He and the twelve returned to Bethany, where they'd spend the night

The next morning as they were leaving, Jesus felt a bit hungry

On the way out, He saw a fig tree, all leafy and green

He approached it to see if He could find a fig

But none could be seen

I'm hungry the Lord said

Because you've not supplied my need

No man here after, from your branches will feed

The next morning, He went back to the Temple
There were merchants buying and selling goods
And Jesus cursed them all
He turned over their tables, and threw them from their stalls
My house is a house of prayer, for it is written
You've turned it into a den of thieves
For this you all should be smitten
The scribes and the priests heard the accusations He had made
And they wanted to destroy Him, but were too afraid
Because the people were astonished by the doctrine He was teaching
And even more, at the miracles He performed
And the stories He was preaching
The next morning, when they left the city
Peter noticed the tree, where no figs were found
From its leaves to its roots, it had withered to the ground
Have faith in God is what the Lord would say
For three years that tree bore no fruit
That's reason enough to take it away
Whatever problems that come your way
Speak to it in My name, and it cannot stay
Believe in your heart, and do not doubt
Whatsoever you speak continually shall come about
And when you pray, forgive all who've offended you
And your father in heaven will forgive your trespasses too
When they came again into Jerusalem
The chief priest, the scribes, and elders sought to challenge Jesus again
So, He spoke to them in parables, and used lots of illustrations
This added to their confusion, and increased their frustrations
Try as they might, they couldn't pin Him down
And every time they tried to trap him
The wisdom of God was found

It was now two days before the Passover feast of the unleavened bread
When a woman approached Jesus and poured
expensive perfume over His head
At this, some became indignant, murmuring to one another
Saying, she has wasted expensive oil, it's running on the floor
She could have sold it for maybe three hundred pence
And given it to the poor
Jesus said let her alone
It's not for you to be worrying
She's come ahead of time to anoint My body for burying
Meanwhile Judas Iscariot went to the chief priest
To seek how he may betray Jesus for a financial increase
Now the first day of the Passover had come
So, Jesus sent Peter and John ahead
To prepare the fatted lamb
That they all may be fed
When you enter the city, there shall be a man with a water pot
Follow him to his house and he'll show you the spot
When they arrived where they'd been sent
It was just as He'd said
It was in the guest room of that man's house
Where they'd be fed
They prepared the last supper, and
At the appropriate time Jesus walked in
"I'm pleased to be here with you, and to share our final meal
For soon the hour cometh
And my Blood will be spilled".
Amen

The Last Supper

The disciples sat around the table ready for their meal
When the Lord entered the room, not knowing how to fill
His heart was very heavy, and His eyes were very dim
For He knew out of the twelve, one would betray Him
With all heads bowed, Jesus began saying His grace
simultaneously scanning the room, looking upon each disciple's face
Jesus expressed his fervent desire to share his final meal
For it will be His last, til His blood be spilled
He took a cup and filled it with wine
Saying, until the kingdom comes
He'd not drink again, from the fruit of vine
He broke a loaf of bread into pieces
And gave each disciple some
Saying He'd not eat again
Until the kingdom of God has come
This bread is my body, I freely give for you
And this wine is my Blood, I'll shed that too
Before you eat and drink every day
In remembrance of Me, you should pray
Abruptly, He interrupted his peace
To say what he could no longer hold
Saying, tonight I will be betrayed, by someone from this fold
The men were astonished, as they began to look around
Wondering who the culprit would be

But the answer wasn't found
Jesus leaned forward, to dip into His stew, and Judas did the same
As they retreated, their gaze met
Judas's eyes were filled with shame
Knowing what was to be done
The Lords heart was filled with grief
Judas Iscariot would be the one
It would take a thief
Judas, the time has come for you to depart
Now go, and do what's in your heart
But woe unto you, for the deceit you've worn
For this night it would be better, if you'd never been born
The disciples started gossiping among themselves,
about how Judas would be smitten
Until Jesus said, this night you'll all stumble, because it is written:
"I shall strike the Shepherd, and the sheep will be scattered"
Peter blurted out
Lord no matter what the others do
No matter what they say
I've been by your side til now
And by your side I'll stay
Peter, I'm touch by what you say
Your intent is very kind
But tonight, you'll betray me thrice
Before the cock crows twice
Not so Lord, you I'd never betray
Jesus wanted badly to believe him
Then, just walked away
For He knew what would happen
And there was nothing more to say
They went to the garden of Gethsemane, and all along the way

His soul was becoming exceedingly sorrowful
And He really needed to pray
He told the disciples where to wait
And He went a little further and fell on the ground
With folded hands He prayed, Father if it be possible
Let mercy be found
After one hour He returned, and found none awake
He asked, couldn't you watch for one hour
If only for My sake
Then He went back for another hour
and in the flesh, He prayed the same prayer
Saying, Father, if it be possible have mercy on me
When He returned, the men were sleep again
No matter how hard they tried
Sleep would win
By the third hour Jesus had prayed over into the spiritual realm
And an angel appeared in the sky
And filled Him with Dunamis power, from His Father on high
This time He prayed: My Lord, and my God,
Not My will, but Thy will be done
Now, I'm ready to die
When He came again, the disciples were fast asleep
This time Jesus wasn't upset, for He was the Sheppard
And they were merely sheep
As He began to awaken them, a crowd led by Judas came through the mist
Judas approached Jesus, and greeted him with a kiss
As the crowd gathered around
Two guards apprehended Jesus from the rear
One of the disciples drew a sword and cut off the guard's ear
Jesus reattached it
And beckoned them not to fight

He asked, have you come against Me, as against a robber in the night?
They took Jesus before the chief priest
For testimonies to be heard
When He agreed that He was the Christ
The crowd didn't need to hear another word
Persecute Him, Persecute Him, Persecute Him
Meanwhile, Peter was in the courtyard warming by the fire
Twice a woman accused him of being a disciple
And twice he called her a liar
And the third time she accused him, he began to swear
I tell you I don't know the man
And that I do declare
No sooner had he said it
Through the crowd the Lord heard Peter, and their eyes met
Immediately, Peter remembered what Jesus had said
And this was a moment, he'd never forget
That evening the crowd mocked Jesus, slapped Him
And spat in His face
They rent His clothes, while tugging and pulling
And mocking Him in disgrace
The next morning, they took Him to Pontius Pilot to be judged
Pilot asked Him to defend Himself, but He refused to budge
Unable to find just cause, Pilot let the crowd decide
After much prompting from the priest
They wanted Him crucified
Crucify Him! Crucify Him!
Pilot demanded a vase of water that he may wash his hands
Saying he'd not be guilty of killing an innocent man
The soldiers led Jesus away while mocking Him even more
They beat Him with a reed, and knocked Him to the floor
Then they twisted a crown of thorns, and jammed it in His head

Oh, King of the Jews save yourself they said
They led Him to a place called Gol'go-tha, and beat Him all the way
Some pleaded, Jesus save yourself, but He had nothing to say
They hung Him on the cross between two transgressors
Prophecy being fulfilled
Then stabbed Him in His side, and His Blood did spill
From the sixth through the ninth hour darkness covered the land
Jesus sounded His final cry,
E-LO-I, -ELO-I, la ma' sa bach-tha ni
It…. Is…. finished….
Amen

I Did It All For You

The rainbow was created as a promise to you
As the firmament returns to the heavens
You'll know, "I Am that I Am" and I've done what I said I'd do
Have you ever stood by the ocean to witness my alpha sunrise?
With mesmerizing colors of pastels
Flung across the morning skies
Or the omega sunsets as the day completes her course
Both speaking volumes, without sound, without voice
With you in mind I created it all
The snow-capped mountains, sand filled valleys, sun drenched deserts
And majestic water falls
With insatiable appetite, and thunderous roar
Cutting gorges through the landscape while rushing to the shores
The winter winds that cut like a knife
Or soft breeze's transporting pollen to start new life
She circles the globe with lighting speed
With currents moving rain, hail, snow, and sleet
Natures balance, so delicate, yet so strong
I've entrusted her to you, and to you she belongs
Droughts, thunder storms, and hurricanes
Tornados, earthquakes, and monsoon rains
Volcano's spew out their bowels, consuming everything in their wake
O yea of little faith, for heaven's sake
She brings hidden treasures from the center of the earth

Brought to the surface, discover her worth
Electrical charges from the lightning bolt
annihilating airborne germs with a single jolt
Horrifying, energizing, electrifying right?
Approach her with fear and trembling, and Godly insight
In her belly, are treasures untold
Only by revelation will you unfold
I've hidden bodies of water beneath the earth for whosoever will
To water their crops, while others wither in the fields
You've only scratched the surface of what awaits you
Eyes have not seen, nor has it entered into the hearts of men
What the Lord has waiting for you, in the palms of his hands.
Amen

Hallelujah

Praise the Lord
Bless His Holy name
Why you'll looking at me like that
If He delivered you from what I've been through
You'd be praising Him too
I'm ok, no it's alright
It's just that when I think of how He keeps me through the day
And comforts me through the night
I spill over with joy, and I can't hold back
All my needs are met, and I have no lack
To keep that to myself would be a shame and a disgrace
It'd be like dishonoring the Lord before His face
So, I say all Glory to God, my father on high
With Holy boldness and selflessness, His name I cry
Your Majesty, your Honor, my Lord, and Grace
You delivered me out of bondage
And elevated me to a higher place
You've loosed me of the things that would hold me back
And steered me on the right course, now I'm on the right track
Thank you, Jesus, for all You've done
Because of You, my journey has begun
Has He done anything for you?
Then don't be a spectator
This is not a sport

This is a way of life
He's our only true support
The promises He made will never change
He can never take them back
They're ours for the asking, that's a fact
If you can believe and never doubt
From the spiritual realm into the natural, it shall come about
Join in with me and let's give Him a praise
And never forsake to do so for the rest of our days
In a radical way, lets lift His name on high
And shout it out with a battle cry
Halleluiah, praise the name of Emmanuel
And may His name forever more, in our bellies dwell.
Amen

In The Valley

When you're walking in the valley
Wear a big smile
Sure, you're confronted with challenges that seems impossible to overcome
But they'll only last a while
Maybe you've been there for weeks, or months, or even years
Seems like it's been such a long time, it's got you filled with fears
Well, listen closely, I got a secret I want to share
Continue to have faith in God, if you dare
You see, Faith is one of the few law's that supersedes time
And when you have no strength left
Faith will help you climb
How long you're in the valley is really up to you
You could concede, and allow the status quo to be you reward
Or you could stick it out under the tutelage of the Lord
He wants to continually speak with you
And tell you where to go, who to see, and what to do
It's that daily grind, that gets you where you can't see
When you're oftentimes only a decision away from where He wants you to be
The lord speaks with a still small voice
And in the valley, you can hear it
Nothing is moving, there is no choice
Even in the air there's no sound
You can hear the blood running through you veins,
and you can hear your heart pound

You know, in your heart is where the spirit of the Lord resides
And His spirit is in there with yours, side by side
So, go ahead, put a huge smile on your face
In the valley, o yes, that's the place
That's where you'll find love, mercy, favor, and grace.
Amen

Is This You?

Today the clouds are bleeding red
And the earth is filled with smoke
Latent genius inside of you, lies dormant and without hope
You could have been, and done, and shared so much more
Instead, lethargy found a resting place just inside your door
Your imagination took you places that only you could go
Gave you ideas and exploits to take to the world
Things that only you could show
Now, today has been cancelled and it's too late
You dreamed the dreams, but failed to act, now emptiness is your fate
The band has played their last song, and you're left to sing alone
Surely it could have been different, if you had only known.

The Spirit Man

When wisdom speaks
Don't listen with your head
Turn inward
Listen with your spirit instead
Train yourself now, while in your youth
For out of the content of your heart, comes all truth
Understanding is not in your head
Its revelation coming through your spirit instead
If the message stops in your head
It'll just be another pebble in the sand
You can obtain knowledge from books
But wisdom doesn't come from man
The Lord made sure of that
You can't hide His revelations under a hoody or a hat
He said He'd send you a comforter
In your belly, He'd hide
Free from contamination, He'd reside
Your spirit man is the real you
He communes with the Father
As your prayers go through
There's your secret hiding place
And only you can enter in
It's free from frustration, confusion, and all manner of sin
A deeper revelation of the principal of two or three touching to agree

And having what they say
It isn't necessarily you and another man
You alone can have what you say
Oh yes you can
The Holy Spirit, and your spirit resides in your heart
When you get your soul to line up with those two
Whatever you continually believe, will come through
Your soul is the decider of your choices, the guardian of your emotions
And the determiner of what you think
You can't rely on it alone
To many of its decisions really stink
So, come on, discipline your soul to line up with your spirit
So you'll have what you say
Then self confidence and assurance will have you walking boldly every day
Wisdom is a principal thing
Where ever you are, you can hear her sing
From the mountain tops to the valleys below
You can hear her voice wherever you go
She leads with words of inspiration
With a voice capable of confounding the nations
Understanding follows her with the melody
With intonation, pitch, and harmony
They take their que from knowledge of the written word
Wherein the voice of the Lord can readily be heard
Listen quietly and be quick to hear
Hide what you've heard in your heart, and it will erase all fear
Fear is a dreadful thing, a crippler that stunts your growth
Impairs your vision, and causes you to fail
It's a deception from old slue foot
Straight from the pit of hell
It's nothing more than False Evidence Appearing Real

Whose design is to destroy, to mutilate, and to kill
So, when wisdom knocks at your door
Open wide and let her in
Lift your countenance, open your arms, and greet her with a grin
And when she opens her mouth, and begin to sing
Be quick to hear, and slow to speak
Listen to what she has to say
And hide whatever you heard in your heart
And it'll be there to stay
And when the time will come, you may never know
You need to give no thought to the directions in which the wind will blow
In fact, give no thought for tomorrow, it's sufficient unto itself
Because the treasures you've hidden in your heart is waiting on the shelf
And there it will be until its occasion arise
In that hour
Her voice will make a grand entrance; she will
come on the crest of a thunder bolt
And out of your mouth her truths will jolt
With power and authority that comes from on high
From whence it came your head will never know
It'll pour out as revealed word
And set a standard and a presence from which you've never heard
And you'll wonder, where did that come from?
Man, what a Word!
Amen

Printed in the United States
By Bookmasters